NEW WORK 1971
revisited

new work 1971

New Work 1971
revisited

A Poetry Chapbook
by
Jack B. Rochester

Joshua Tree Press LLP
Boston

Published by Joshua Tree Press LLP
5 Hollow Lane
Lexington, Massachusetts 02420
https://joshuatreeinteractive.com
jack.rochester@mac.com

ISBN: 979-8-9874421-2-8 (softcover print only)

This book is distributed to the trade through Ingram/Spark and may be purchased or special-ordered from traditional and independent booksellers such as Apple, Amazon, Barnes & Noble, Bertrams, Booktopia, Kobo, or Waterstone.

For Susan Horsefield

Introduction

In 1971, when my wife at the time and I were college students, we collaborated on a book with my poetry and her art. It was the purest labor of love: love for one another and for our creative pursuits. We assembled her drawings and my poems and published this book, *New Work 1971*, on our college English Department's mimeograph machine. That, itself, was also a labor of love.

I don't recall how many copies we printed, but it was likely only a few which we gave to our parents and a few close friends. To my knowledge, I possess the last known copy. For years I've wanted to republish it, but never gave myself the time or permission. The *New Work 1971 revisited* you now hold in your hands is the second limited edition of this work, using today's technologies.

All of these poems were written in the late 1960s and very early '70s, as the title date implies. Some were published in small literary and college magazines, back when we didn't keep track of our literary kudos quite as well as we do these days. I added "September Love Song" which has always stood out for me as one of my finest works, so it deserves to be in this chapbook. Written in 1967, its original title was "February Love Song" and it made its way into my first novel, *Wild Blue Yonder*, written by the main character, Nathaniel Hawthorne Flowers. I had to change February to September so it would complement the novel's narrative.

Other than that, not a single word in any of these poems has been changed for this new edition, although I added a title to one which didn't have one (as several others do not). The first edition contained 19 poems; by including "February Love Song" the total is 20. To my mind, it now has a kind of *sophrosyne*, since it's also the 20th book of my writing to be published (not counting the original *New Work 1971*). I've always loved Sophrosyne, the Greeks goddess so-named for balance, proportion, moderation, and symmetry. Like a good poem.

I tapped a willow sprig
Upon the chrysalis-mirrored pond,
Tap-tap-tap Tiresias at the font,
Faint signals to send my message,
Ask my question

And the water replied in echo
With the stillness of the imploding cosmos
Crying in a thousand
Diffusing
Circles.

Maiden Mother

Quietly magnificent, she sits alone,
Sad eyes seeing visions in her mind,
Hands holding dreams she'll never materialize;
Burnished hair tumbles over carelessly naked
shoulders —
Ric-rac racing across phosphorescent waters —
To shroud her faith in the morning;
Her stomach alive: a soft, sensual globe of
anticipation
Resting heavily between her thighs;
Backsliding youth now obliterated, lost to a
moment;
Her life this life, at once rebirth and
reincarnation,
A universe ne'er explored; a spirit now sent
To a placenta she knows
From the tv doctor shows.

What made the day so patient,
Made the sun wish to linger
Just beyond the apex of its flight?
What constrained the minute hand
Of the clock which carried people
Through the chore of living?

Surely all the days he spent
With her had never seemed so long
And now, to walk and wait and think
Of eight years' commitment to
The difficult task of marriage
And the more painful matter

Of learning to live with oneself,
Of learning to reckon with a quirk
Of nature, which was a sportster's
Delight but a husband's nemesis,
Carrying that terrible craving
In one's loins, finding a degree

Of solace in a union one wished,
Not of necessity but of nature,

To be spiritual and intellectual:
Pursuing life at full gallop,
Lost in distraction, high on drugs,
Eventually leaving these itinerant

Fancies for the calm and reverent
Life of the country town and the
Wider world of nature, face asweat
With the gut-heaving satisfaction
Of building one's home, and garden
Food, and mellowing of two hearts;

That this growing had struck deeper, that
The gift of life was still within and
Had caressed his wife; that now, all
Fears could be forgotten, all strength
Was in their souls, all sins could be forgiven,
And her atonement was his child;

The time of doctor-seeing, the plans
Forming and growing in her womb and
In the nursery he was building, life
Becoming good, no, great and better
Yet but still a small doubt nagging,
An omen of the past still leaden within

Until it burned his brain and drove him
To this clandestine meeting with the m.d.
And his lab; the specimen in testing,
The time so slow in passing and the face
Before him saying, sadly, how it was no use;
Infidelity no mask to him who is betrayed.

Oh, Amchitka*, how sad
That today your soul and substance
Was rent up for man's amusement;
What gives that politician, that man
To whom reason is necromancy, witchcraft,
The right to ordain your destruction,
You,
So pure and simple? Oh yes, there is
Recompense: you are now a legend, for
These days it only takes a week,
And of course, the local rock station
Exploits your rape with references to
Most anything in general;
But what of your immortality, Amchitka?
What of the pure place from which you came,
What of your virgin expanses, what of the
Evolution of your Eskimo name, and what
Of those who came to name you?
Oh Amchitka, how sad
I am today for you, and how much
My sadness reeks of self-pity.

* https://en.wikipedia.org/wiki/Cannikin

Upon Learning the Kenyon Review Had Ceased Publication After 30 Years, While Browsing In The Library

It was an explosion in that quiet corridor,
Like inflation or the recession
      finally striking home,
Lashing its teeth-tipped whip
Into the spines of my favorite books.

I don't claim to know you, Kenyon College,
Though you've stolen my stamps
      for many years
In the plight to see my words immortalized
On your printed pages, and you know?

I'd like to see them there still, in fondness
For the many years of volume-collecting
      we have done;
Our library is bantam but it's growing fast,
To meet the needs of our growing,
      industrious community.

He stands at the edge of the stage,
A speck of life in silhouette
Against the vast, eternal glare of white
Which is the infinity of movie screen

(Outside, people are milling around
In front of the auditorium, in listless
Anticipation;)

The class sits watching him, hearing
His voice roll out through the lecture hall,
The knell of a discordant bell
Tolling the fate of the course:

(Outside, people fingering their dollars
While the film is being threaded for
The People's Benefit;)

The Department, the College, does not foresee
An allocation of funds for the class
And since, without films, there's no sense
To it, the students are given a choice:

(Outside, three People's Cinemas, seven
People's groups, two College Departments
Showing films)

The class will go underground;
Funds to be raised in private, The
Friends of the Class to procure films
So the course can be completed;

(Outside: Chaplin, Scarface, Bergman,
Citizen Kane, but the gap
A dollar wide)

New Wave lost, drowned in a sea
Of confusion and bureaucracy; the filmic
Pattern a ghost of what it could have been
Now haunting a B-film lecture hall.

Professor Bobby broke his arm
The other day because, he said,
Of doing his part for ecology;
His department fellows bore the shame
With less compassion than the students
He told his wife who, incensed,
Began a letter to the news;
Poor Molly, daughter of despair, who shouldered
All care for her mate's esteem, Molly,
Who worked for five long, tedious years
While Bobby garnered three degrees
From NorthSouth Central State; Molly,
Who was not abashed to tell
The faculty wives their clubby stuff
Was sham for lauding petty claims
Their husbands sought for fame;
Bob had thought a course or two
In disciplines relevant to the new
Culture scene would do poor Molly good
But she seemed only versed to see
The entangling world of coed's thighs
Which threatened scholarly pursuits;
So, relegated to a homey role
She chatted about other things
And hostessed visits of Bob's "group"

Of students who felt that his thoughts
Held special meaning they could see,
The field of English what it was,
A den of pythons, packrats, wolves,
And he a man who had to share,
To teach a message lacking self
Had welcomed meetings of the "group"
For sharing thoughts which were too new
For credence in the classroom world;
Bob turned them on to counterthoughts
And they reciprocated in their way
To move the spirit and the mind
In ways poor Molly only glimpsed
But never caused her stay away;

And now the "group" has sent a card
Expressing their condolence for
The fall Bob took upon his bike
While pedaling to school;
The doctor said "a hairline break"
And hoped the cast was not a chore
And cautioned Bob about his youth
And what was lack thereof;
Professor Bob has thus returned
To driving now, and almost feels relief;

He won't admit it was the street —
Says carelessness had caused the spill —
And if his peers find fault with him
It's something he should just accept
And not permit their petty fears
To feed upon his own.

INDICTMENT

He was obviously a man of letters;
Perls and Piaget focused in mandalas
Which spun, in art and thought,
Through the vortex of his life cycle;

I looked into his face
And his hair seemed great waves
Of black water, foaming against
His psyche in a vast storm, roaring

"Well, like I can dig what he's
Laying down, but he doesn't make it
In terms of what's really happening,
You know, seeing Om," he gestured,

"And I just can't get into it,
I mean, it's the dude's trip but
It's not where I'm at, and, well it's
Just now not where I'm at. But it's cool."

And he leaned back in his chair
And lit his Danish pipe
And grinned at me
In a most ingratiating way.

APOLOGY TO **W. H.**

I used to think that college was
A place where scholars tested
The meaning of metaphor,
What truth was there invested;

But lately what I find is that
The greatest test of all
Is finding Truth in "I _feel_ that . . ."
And "Isn't school a ball?"

Placation is the Now Approach
And not arousing ire
For, threaten kids with discipline
They'll likely start a fire

And not the flame of knowledge light,
For this is learning's twist:
The sensory experience
Is all that may exist.

The form has lost its shapeliness
And content is a-lacking;
Ideas now are Happenings,

And critics need the sacking.

If this seems disagreeable,
Not fun, like freely freaking,
Then disregard my office hours,
My classes and my teaching.

AT THE URINAL

Believe me when I tell you
I've been in some of the world's most
Notable public restrooms
And Mark Twain's comment about men never
Looking one another in the eye
Notwithstanding . . .
I've still cast a look around
And find it difficult to understand
The man who always remembers
To wash his hands
But never remembers
To pull the handle.

CAN YOU PLAY IT TO RAGTIME?

I was born in forty-four,
A product of the last great war;
My schooldays were the shorter night,
No less intense, of Korean fight;

When old enough to be aware
I learned of the atomic scare;
In college days, locked in my digs
I sweated out the Bay of Pigs.

When all else failed I did my time,
A four-year sentence, unsublime;
Yet I was grateful not to hear
Folks fight, except for German beer.

But now I'm out and still I see
These battles off the China Sea;
From war, it seems, there's no surcease;
So where, my friends, can we find peace?

AND WE ALL KNOW THE ANSWER.

In season all I would commend
Seems tendered to an icy tomb;
I think I think a bit too much
And tempt that precipice of doom;

Lamenting springtime's soulful fires,
The sun the eye of all mankind;
The planets turn in rhythmic orbs;
How is it I'm so awfully blind?

The House-Razing

It takes man to smell the smoke
To check smudge pots, feel the sun,
To at evening light the lamps;
Once a spark, a chinking of flint
And the night grew less dark for
Our ancestors, but not less fearful.

I am ever fearful of the night;
Afraid of darkness, afraid when alone,
Afraid of dancing hearthstone embers
In dreams that never, ever end
Yet not afraid to believe again
In things that magic once forestalled;

I recall an ancient witch's death
Upon a childhood night, the quiet
Fear of passing from dream to dream;
And now those fears have come back
To mock me, tiny sparks in blackness
Turn walls to tinder, in my sleep.

The world's profane, insane.
I left the incubus of self-made breakfasts
        and the sneers of separating children
To find that most all things one comes
        to expect of life
        in one's most pitiful moments
Do, in fact, begin at home.

There are one anothers:
        one cries for love,
        wishing to love oneself; or,
One never cries, never,
Making others cry for themselves;
        One, finally, in abject despair,
        Does exactly as others wish
And passes sentence on his soul and sanity.

Flinging the dangling albatross 'round back
So, he won't have to look at it so much
And then one day, a new day
        just like all the rest
        makes one, once more,
A believer in a vision beyond this plane.

This plane of existence, this time
Of futility which lauds frustration
As the means of creative fulfillment
        (The new rites of passage);
        and one begins again
        to need one anothers,
Becomes hopeful that certain chapters
Can now be completed in one's book of life,
Becomes aware that one's aloneness in life
Is a sham reordering of thwarted needs,
        stifled screams,
        arid sobs in the night;

And from the touch-and-tango
Of the seeds of one's own destiny,
The growth and permutation of new life
        to be shared, loved,
        comes the dawning gift
Of the evolving, recurring pattern of it all,
The utter stupidity, now a little funny,
        now a little pitiful,
        now a little painful
As it happens with another
        called your own
        and one begins again

To need one another, and one begins
Again to need one another and
One begins again to begin again.

SAGITTARIUS

Like nature's lightning striking,
The peal of cosmic power,
Sent piercing sacred bower
Conjugal voices praising

The thrust now like a beacon
Caresses in the ocean;
Dancing waves roll wildly
'Neath the noble archer's arrow.

CHANSON À SUZANNE

Ma chérie est belle comme un jour d'été ;
Le matin, elle prépare le thé et les croissants
Et je suis sur le patio ; J'aime sa robe
Et le ciel, sa beauté est comme un oiseau.

L'après-midi, elle devient papillon,
tout juste sorti du cocon de l'amour, et transforme
notre maison en un château, propre et lumineux ;
Puis elle prend son pinceau et peint sur la toile

Et je la regarde
En secret et je vois la petite métamorphose
Encore et encore, je vois mon amour se transformer

La chose simple, la chose quotidienne, en splendeur
Seulement pour que je voie son aspect sensuel, son aspect spirituel,
Car je suis le seul à boire à travers les yeux de ma chérie.

The question remains: either to
Submit to the rationale or
Let insanity be my bridle;
I've ceased to try to ferret out
A word here, a flashing cinder
There, only to turn the steed
Which is me loose, carry you
Across the pastures of my dreams,
Twisting, pawing, splashing, cavorting,
In the winedrops, in the wordstorms,
In placid, hidden dens only we know,
Seeking, ever seeking, yet caught in
The act of knowing nothing is ever
      really known,
      for sure . . .
Spurtip touches flank, and I
Feel the blood thump in my heart;
Fingers tangle my mane, and
My nostrils flare, fill with you;
My eyes see too widely, nature at odds
And focus is elusive in days of days;
Were my torso tomorrow manlike
My loins would still carry you
In a like fashion, my task your
Delight and my delight our flight;

Freedom the bit between my teeth,
Clenched or gagged upon, yet
Something ever known, always
Filled with something lingering,
Elusive as those three words which
Often bring the color to your cheek,
Or turn your skin more pale
Than ever you would wish; I
Find a pattern in my hoofprints
No one can define; the only
Surcease we are allowed is never
         to count backward
         or, too much, look down.

February Love Song

The second hand of my watch is counting
as the minutes since our parting pass by;
Pale violet light from streetlamps illuminates the
fog
and my feet scuff the pavement.

Minutes turned hours mark the passing of my
recollections
of our words, our touching:
Dim now, elusive, like the scent of perfume
behind your ear
lost to the cold kiss of the wind.

Few cars pass by as I walk away from you,
you, now asleep under covers in your quiet room;
My senses tingle at the thought and my jacket
clings to me, as if to remind . . .

The silence screams my separateness:
fog clutters, obfuscates my mind;
All I have of you I clutch to me, hold fast,
our bond in the worldly, lonely night.

I hold the passing of time immobile with you;
your image walks with me into the night.
The light will ever be in front of me,
the fog lifted, in your three-syllable good-bye.

I stop sometimes now, to look back;
Something rare, like glazed embers in
The pipe bowl, seeking eternity in
Burnt ashes, not unlike moments that
Come to pass and slip away, come
to pass
and slip away . . .
Moments when snow crunched under
The steady heel of cowboy boots, firm
Shoulders cut soft edges in
The cold, cruel plains-winds,
Searching with slitted eyes, passing
Down slick sidewalks, finding respite
In the 11:00 classroom; all too new,
All too vague for sensibility, only
Raw mental faculties and a sense
Of the poetic — no names, no titles,
No movements to sustain it — but
All accolades in the gentle man
Whose fingers desperately squeezed
Trembling cigarettes, who suggested
California, I not knowing why,
But at the time the quest was everywhere;
It came crashing in upon me one night,

One night too many; respite from the
Long late-hour conversations, respite
From dormitory telephones and silly,
Frivolous affairs that chased white
Rabbits until they were senseless;
It came to pass, the snow asleep
In window dormers, some indefinite
Being alive inside some aspect of myself
Which was all too new to express,
Even in the journal I was writing
For my yet-unborn heirs, it came to pass
That the being exploded out in a torrent
Of tears, and I found myself alone.

How does one find oneself alone? It's
Not like naming of parts, though we
Are led to discover possession of mind,
Stomach, hands and hearts, much like
A chicken found dead in the grocery store,
But still and none the less, I'm whole.
I would like to tell you how whole
I am but you would attribute it to
Being possessed, for equilibrium today is,
I am told, unsane, but no one possesses
Me but Me. Only if you defy the structure

Of my symbolism can you credit me with
Possession. There are those who would
Possess, Zimmerman's Masters of War
Ringing through long hallways, not unlike those
Passed but now possessed, bound into a hideous
Contract which was on the Law itself but
Never seen, yet signed, no lawyer present.
For slavery, we are told, is no longer right;
Masters of War, the Mind Cripplers
Of a generation, souls shaved off with locks
Of hair, hearts trampled beneath the heels
Of thirty-three recruits on a barren, empty,
Meaningless Texas parade ground: divestment
Is the means of enlightenment, denial the road
To truth, brutality the only lesson learned,
Brutality never confined to barbed-wire
Battlegrounds. There are no Penal Colonies
There are no concentration camps, there
Are no restrictions in the soft, warm, deserted
space
A bullet makes in the brain; there is no
Agony like the agony of wishing to be free
To do nothing (fifteen minutes in the
Border lockup, the panic of turning the
Handle and finding the door open) and doing
nothing

About it; the boredom opening skyways of
Contemplation, back alleys becoming freeways
And dreams becoming a series of unending,
Repeating escapades that tell stories, stupid
With high school drama until the idea
Grips with tentacles and won't let go,
Won't forsake the quest for any intermission,
won't
Wait for the convenience of right time
And with the commander's approval (and
Blessing, of course, for Education is
Sacred when it doesn't Interfere with Duty) a
new march
Begins.

Through a new city, one seeking nothing
For that was vogue then, perhaps is now,
The city accustomed to young men and their
quests,
And their means of seeking; not music (but
Of course it was there too, in abundance
On the street, so many arms clutching
The music they would play that night in
Half-dark rooms, the music that would take
Their souls and sensibilities and gently

Lave them in lost chords and smiling,
Elusive words until, until that same music spun
Them in a mad vortex that stopped mid-
Something;) nor woman, nor the excitement
Of the streets or theater but the subtle
World of eyes that talked and matchboxes
Without matches and the thrill of a secret,
A secret which promised a pure path, if
Not an answer, to the quest; a pure path
a pure path
which denied the Masters
and the brutality
and celebrated innocence without tears
and assuaged need that would never, ever be met
and provoked laughter and bonds
and that only brothers who share a secret
understood the meaning of
A harmless thing, of course, all knew
And packed a dialect and set of facts
Which allayed all levels of doubt, at
Least to those who knew, and never did it
Lead to other things, perhaps to any
Thing; but that was still to learn,
And even if there was no proof, to
See significant where none had been before

Seemed proof enough to me that, still,
There was indeed a quest;
I pursued it joyously, through City
Streets, through German forests, on wheels,
On Andalusian islands, on foot and through
The distorting, troubling canals of the moon I
worshipped
In the deepest, most significant pain
My mind could ever claim, and
The moon was ever-faithful to my quest,
Shedding no light to see clearly by, no
Shadows by which to trace my steps,
Only the colors that sparkled and twisted
Behind closed eyes, drumming in my
Insane eardrums, like dying stars,
Leading me into caverns of doom
That never knew the light.
And in those bleakest caverns,
In those most hideous dreams that
Coursed through me day and night
A moment, single and at rest,
Showed true to what had ceased
To be the quest but only the
Monotonous cycle of days which
Careened one into another, a form

In all the obliterate formlessness, who
Took me back to the place of my roots
And caused me to open my eyes
For the first time to the sunlight.
It was a place where trees speak,
Where stories are told which have endings
Where one thing leads to another and
Follow to conclusions which the haze
Of conflict doesn't obfuscate, obliterate,
Where ideas seek truth, not truth seeking
Different modes of individuality, and
Where the quest finds form, and even words
and the word is love;

and I shall quest no longer,
and I shall not try to find my parts,
and I shall not forsake my path,
and I shall not seek manifestation,
and I shall love ignorance, for it leads to
knowledge,
and I shall not make excuses, nor blame;
I shall only love my quest,
and I shall only love my love.

It's getting later;
Dusk turns dawn in countless revolutions
And I must be on. Vague symbols
Emerge, but I must be on. What
I seek is a chair with arms too enclosing
Rich velvet too comforting, reflection
Being too idle a gesture now, when
There are so many explorations ahead;
I must go on.

Lessons seek examples, and that
Self-seeking harkens me back too much. Let us
never
Deny our past, yet let us never seek it;
Make my mortality a drum to thump,
I'll not splay invectives to discredit it
But a timid hand never reaches far
And I must be on.

Yes, give me timelessness; nothing else
Could put me off this mad wheel, stop
My need to believe in you; I know, I
Deny too much, but troublesome images

In the cogwheels give me too much reason.
The blessing, some kind pattern in
The velvet fabric, seeks equanimity
In this digression, and it would be
Unfair, were it not so true, that
Curse and contentment are of the same mold
Too many times an urge to scream
At Dante, pummel Kafka and
Talk endless hours with Blake, to
Walk through public artways with
Her, closer than a footstep, pressing
Thought to thought in an alliance
Unsteeped in damp locks, only eyes,
And were the combination of the one
To become
Then its expression would be nevermore
Than before, a totality of touch to create
A universe, not a word, nor a brushstroke;

But I must be on, you see,
For this is once again where I have been
And once again too much one thought
In seeking, thought sought; I'm sated,
For I have no longer such a journey, for
There's perfection in a human sense

And that's all one can ask: it wants
No more a rapture than repose, and
In its perfect moment I rise again to
Find a way to put it into words
For you see, I must be on;
It's in my nature
In my lifeblood.
And now I must be on.

SPECIAL THANKS TO:

Kristin Thornburgh for her excellence and diligence in reviewing, editing and typing the new manuscript for this reprinted edition. She had to work with the last known copy of the original chapbook, not an easy task reading 50-year-old purple mimeograph printing. It was a considerable effort and I'm grateful. https://www.linkedin.com/in/kristin-thornburgh-6012851b1/

Sophie Hanks, my partner in publishing, for the page design, layout and typesetting. https://sophiehanks.com/

Shehab Hossain for sharing his extraordinary long-exposure photograph, "Lake Powell, Arizona," as our cover art. The landscape was illuminated by ambient light from the stars overhead. https://www.imaginoor.com/

Melanie Marston of Marston Creative for the new cover design. https://marstoncreative.com/

Antony Wootten, for his Kindle Direct Publishing and Ingram/Spark publishing expertise. https://antonywootten.co.uk/

Tim Knickerbocker at Books International for the handsome limited-edition hardcover edition. https://www.booksintl.com/

About Jack B. Rochester

Jack in 1972

As a college student Jack B. Rochester longed to see a book with his name on the cover. *New Works 1971 Revisited* makes it 20 books and counting. He launched his career as a business book editor, guiding several hundred authors' books into print. In 1983, he launched his startup professional writing and editorial services company, Joshua Tree Interactive, and saw the publication of the bestseller *The Naked Computer*. His extensive writing in business and high tech included three college textbooks, ending with his nonfiction swan song/last hurrah, the internationally acclaimed *Pirates of the Digital Millennium* (both TNC and PODM co-authored with his brother-from-another-mother John Gantz).

In 2007, Jack turned to writing fiction. His Nathaniel Hawthorne Flowers literary trilogy – *Wild Blue Yonder*, *Madrone*, and *Anarchy* – was published by Wheatmark. A distinctly different novel, *Bridge Across the Ocean*, (Brilliant Light Publishing/Media, 2021), followed. JackBoston.com, his innovative website, displays his writing career in both words and images. His books and many shorter works are available in print, e-book and Audible formats.

He's the co-founder of The Fictional Café, an online 'zine publishing fiction, poetry, creative nonfiction, fine art, photography, and fiction-based podcasts for 1500 subscribers in 45 countries. Two Fictional Café anthologies, *The Strong Stuff: The Best of Fictional Café*, volumes I and II, present the first ten years of the site's publishing on behalf of its Coffee Club membership.

Jack earned a Master's degree in Comparative Literature from California State University at Sonoma. He grew up in South Dakota and Wyoming and spent many years on the Left Coast. These days he and his Darling wife spend summers in the Boston area and winters on Florida's Space Coast. An avid cyclist, he owns five bicycles. He likes to say no moss grows beneath his feet.

JACK'S NOVELS

U.S. AIR F
WILD
BLUE
YONDER
A NOVEL
JACK B. ROCHESTER

It's 1965 and Airman Nathaniel Hawthorne Flowers goes, not to Vietnam, but to Germany and straight into a military Catch-22. His assignment: write stories for the *Stars and Stripes* newspaper that will never see print. Nate's adventure deepens as he and his fellow troops try to understand why they're there, the military mindset, and the massive social disruption roiling 1960's America. Existential, psychedelic, funny, and laced with rock 'n' roll, *Wild Blue Yonder* is the story of Nate's quest for personal and spiritual values while trying to learn the meaning of family, friendship, and the love of the girl he left behind.

"Jack Rochester's novel is a convincing account of what it must have been like to be very young in the Sixties, feeling a bit lost and alienated from family, trying to stay sane in the arbitrary and often absurd world of the military, while the controversial war was raging and the counterculture bloomed. (Some of the most engaging scenes are vivid accounts of the Haight-Ashbury, a be-in in Golden Gate Park with Timothy Leary, and a first encounter with LSD.)" ~ X. J. Kennedy

THE SECOND NATHANIEL HAWTHORNE FLOWERS NOVEL
MADRONE
Winner
Jack B. Rochester

The year is 1969. After an interminable four years under the boot of the US military, twenty-four-year-old Nathaniel Hawthorne Flowers is ready for his real life to begin. His plans are straightforward: spend as much time as he can with his girlfriend, Jane Chandler, finish college, and become a writer. But when Nate is denied admission to UC Santa Cruz, he decides that a bachelor's degree isn't necessary for the path he's laid out for himself. He can learn about literature on his own, and he'll have more time to write if he isn't in a classroom. Yet when a once-in-a-lifetime opportunity presents itself, even Nate is tempted by the allure of conventionally defined success. Picking up where *Wild Blue Yonder* left off, *Madrone* inspires us to consider how far we'll go to remain true to ourselves.

Madrone was chosen for the Best Literary Fiction Award by the Independent Publishers of New England in 2016.

"It's an artist's story. Music and love are not all . . . but those moments when we believe they are? Right here." - Hugo Burnham

The Third Nathaniel Hawthorne Flowers Novel
ANARCHY
AUTOGRAPHED COPY
Jack B. Rochester

Set amid the tumultuous days of American dissent against the Vietnam War and worldwide student protests, *Anarchy* sees Tim Rosencrantz, from *Wild Blue Yonder*, reappear in Nate Flowers's life, spreading evil and disruption. Tim is now a full-fledged member of Weatherman. Bent on bombing America to its senses, he wants Nate at his side. Nate, although anti-war and intellectually sympathetic, is reluctant to participate in Tim's anarchy - until, that is, Tim blackmails him. Unknown to Nate, the FBI has Tim and Crystal, his naive teenage moll, under surveillance. As Tim and Crystal plot the bombing of a Bank of America, everyone realizes this cannot end well - but just how badly they cannot imagine.

"Nate is now a published writer with a reputation to polish and a terrific girl friend (Jane Chandler) to nourish. Toward the middle of the book Nate gives a reading of a short story called "Biting Through," a reference to the *I-Ching* hexagram 21. The story is the caramel at the center of this delicious book. It is, of course, about the destruction anarchy can wreak. In a rather clever way it draws the line between the two characters, setting up the conflict, which draws many of the secondary characters into the turmoil." ~ Rob Swigart

BRIDGE
ACROSS THE OCEAN
澎湖跨海大
A NOVEL
JACK B. ROCHESTER

Set in today, *Bridge Across the Ocean* is the story of four New England entrepreneurs who founded Smithworks, a high-end custom bicycle maker. Now partner Shieh-Seng "Luke" Lin has invented the Spinner, the most innovative bicycle drive in history, which produces and stores its own energy without batteries. A week before they are to leave for Taipei, Taiwan, to license it to Joyful Bike, the world's largest bicycle maker, Luke is killed by a hit-and-run driver. The remaining three persevere, but at Tokyo's Narita International Airport are set upon by two Japanese intellectual property thieves. The cyclists are pursued to Taipei and a game of espionage-counterespionage ensues, alongside a cross-cultural romance between Jedediah Smith and Jung-Shan Zheng.

"A Taiwanese travelogue filled with an array of international characters, philosophies on living, and bits of Confucius, Thomas Jefferson, and the Tao thrown in. The cross-cultural differences are fascinating and the scenery descriptions lovely, enticing, and inviting, making Taiwan a place I'd like to see." ~ Mark Greenside